Twenty to Make

Celebration Cake Pops

Paula MacLeod

First published in Great Britain 2012

Search Press Limited
Wellwood, North Farm Road,
Tunbridge Wells, Kent TN2 3DR

Text copyright © Paula MacLeod 2012

Photographs by Paul Bricknell at
Search Press Studios

Photographs and design copyright
© Search Press Ltd 2012

ISBN 978 1 84448 763 9

Suppliers
If you have difficulty in obtaining any of the
materials and equipment mentioned in this book,
then please visit the Search Press website for
details of suppliers: www.searchpress.com

Printed in Malaysia

Dedication

*This book is dedicated to my loyal and
loving husband, Steve, to my children
Glen and Stephanie for all their ongoing
encouragement and support over the years,
and to Dee and Pete for Abbi-Rose and
Ella May.*

Acknowledgements
I would like to thank the whole team at
Search Press for all their hard work. A
special thanks to Roz for offering this title
to me, to Ali for all her help, support
and guidance, Marrianne for her
attention to detail and Paul for his
magical photograhy.
A very special thank you to Shailesh and
Pat at Knightsbridge PME Ltd who have
greatly assisted with both equipment and
materials consistently throughout this
book. And also to Lisa without whom
this book would not have happened.
Thank you.

*You are invited to visit the
author's website
www.creativecakecompany.com*

Publisher's Note
If you would like more information about
baking and sugarcraft, try
Decorated Cupcakes, Search Press, 2009 by
Frances McNaughton or *Decorated Cookies*,
Search Press, 2010 by Lisa Slatter, both in
the Twenty to Make series.

Contents

Introduction

The first novelty cake I made was for a stall at my daughter's pre-school when she was just three years old. I remember it brought great delight to many and set me along a journey of creative learning and fun, which I hope to share with you now in cake pop form! Whether you are making for a cake stall, birthday or wedding, your cake pops will take centre stage!

I truly believe cake creations of any kind should always be fun, enjoyable and achievable to make and create, but ultimately delicious and exciting to eat. These bite-sized pieces of yumminess are no exception; there are projects to suit all occasions and all abilities, from single pops for a beginner to bi-pops for the more adventurous, with scope to adapt and personalise, and they all make great cake toppers too.

The recipe and techniques are easy to follow, and there is no need to bake. The piping techniques are basic, but can be made more intricate as you grow in confidence. All the ingredients are easy to source from online suppliers, good sugarcraft retailers and supermarkets. I have chosen ingredients to make life easy, such as the ready-coloured melting candy, which is also readily available.

Don't be afraid to experiment with your own recipes, as this is a good way to develop your own ideas and styles, but if you are new to cake pops, the projects in this book are a great way to get you started.

Opposite
*Meet the pops!
A small selection of
single and pops and
bi-pops ready to inspire
your creativity.*

Materials

Cake pop mixture The basis for all the pops; made by following the recipe on page 48.

Ready-coloured melting candy For securing the cake mixture to the lollipop stick and for covering the pop.

100% vegetable fat This thins down and smooths the melting candy mixture if it is too thick.

Buttercream/frosting Used to hold the crumbled cake together and also for piping.

Piping gel Used to pipe on details, but can also be used to secure sprinkles and modelling paste to the pops.

Food colouring To colour the buttercream.

Edible lustre spray Used to add glitter and sparkle.

Edible dusts These add highlights and are applied with a brush.

Edible ink pens For adding details.

Modelling paste Used to add details to the pops as it is stronger than sugarpaste.

Sprinkles, edible pearl dragrees, ready-made candy sweets Used throughout the book to make construction easier; use ones of your choice and alter the designs for variety.

Icing sugar To prevent the modelling paste from sticking when rolled out.

Rice paper Can be used on some projects as an edible alternative to pop wraps.

Tools

Pop wraps Used as decoration in some projects and attached to the pop or stick.

Elastic band For securing the pop wraps to the sticks.

Lollipop and cookie sticks (non-plastic) The plastic variety are not recommended for any of the projects in this book. The cookie sticks are a little stronger and used with a weightier pop.

Kitchen paper Useful when using edible dust.

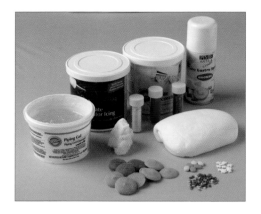

Measuring spoons For measuring the correct amount of mixture for your pops. You will need to use these for each project.

Palette knife For shaping and trimming the pops.

Sharp knife For cutting the paste.

Dresden tool Used for marking the paste.

Cutting wheel For cutting out, shaping or adding texture.

Scallop tool For shaping details.

Bulbous cone tool Used to make angled buttonholes on the groom's jacket.

Ball tool Used to indent the paste.

Cutters Heart: 3cm (1⅛in), 2.5cm (1in), 2cm (¾in)

Oval: 7cm (2¾in)

Circle: 5cm (2in), 3.5cm (1⅜in), 3.2cm (1¼in)

Circle (with deep sides): 5cm (2in), 4cm (1½in)

Fluted circle cutter: 2.5cm (1in)

Square: 5cm (2in), 4cm (1½in), 2.6cm (1⅛in), 1.5 cm (½in)

Five petal flower cutter: 7.5cm (3in)

Plungers Heart: 1cm (⅜in), blossom: 1cm (⅜in), 1.3cm (½in), gerbera: 8.5cm (3¼in), star: 1cm (⅜ in)

Ribbon Used for decoration in some projects.

Scriber This can be used to divide paste or create hole marks.

Cocktail sticks Can be used instead of using specially-designed tools to make marks on sugarpaste.

Non-stick 23cm (9in) rolling pin For rolling out the paste.

Non-stick board A good surface to work on the pops.

Smoother Use this when rolling sausage-shapes of paste to remove fingerprints and marks.

Paintbrush Used for applying piping gel and edible dusts.

Soft dusting brush Used for applying edible dusts.

Decorative rolling pin Impresses a design on to the paste when rolled across it.

Marzipan spacers Give an even depth of the cake mixture when rolled out.

Disposable piping bags Used for piping buttercream and the melting candy mixture.

Small scissors For trimming off the end of the piping bag, and useful in all the projects.

Decorative craft scissors For cutting a decorative edge into rice paper.

Tweezers Will make handling dragees and tiny sweets easier.

Piping tubes (various sizes): No. 2, no. 5, no. 17, no. 18, no. 42c.

Greaseproof paper To line the baking tray when chilling the pops to stop them sticking.

Polystyrene block Used for holding the cake pops.

Baking tray To lay pops on to when chilling.

New Year Lanterns

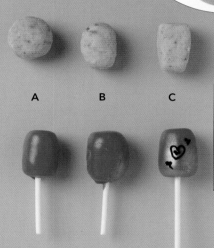

Materials:

Cake pop mixture (see page 48)

Red melting candy

Chocolate (brown) buttercream/frosting

Black food colouring

Edible gold dust or edible
  lustre spray in gold

Lollipop sticks

Tools:

Measuring spoon (tbsp)

Palette knife

Scriber or cocktail stick

No. 2 piping tube

Small scissors

Disposable piping bag

Paintbrush

Polystyrene block

Kitchen paper

A   B   C

'Together'

'Happiness'

'Wealth'

'Harmony'

Instructions:

1 Roll a tablespoon measurement of cake pop mixture into a ball (A) between the palms of your hands. Gently shape to an oval (B) by lightly squeezing between your fingers and thumb. Flatten the base and the top (C) by lightly pressing with a palette knife on to the work surface. Repeat for as many pops as you require and allow them to set by chilling in the fridge.

2 Prepare some red melting candy and secure the lollipop stick to the pop following the technique on page 48. Place into a polystyrene block and chill in the fridge.

3 Dip each lantern pop into the red melted candy (see page 48) and return to the fridge to set.

4 Place a little edible gold dust on to kitchen paper, load a paintbrush with the dust, and remove the excess by tapping the brush over the kitchen paper. Dust lightly over each lantern pop. If using a gold lustre spray, place the chilled pops in a polystyrene block and spray more than one at a time.

5 Choose a design. Use a scriber or cocktail stick to lightly scratch a pattern guideline on to the lantern.

6 Add 2 tablespoons of black food colouring to the chocolate buttercream. Cut off the end of a disposable piping bag and place a no. 2 piping tube inside. Half fill the bag with the prepared buttercream.

7 Place the pop flat on your work surface and touch the piping tube to the pop. Apply pressure to the bag, lift it slightly and allow the line of icing to drop on to the pop to pipe on your design. Stop the pressure and lift away the tip. Tidy up with a paintbrush if necessary. Place in the polystyrene block and leave to dry.

> **Tip!**
>
> When piping, keep the piping tube in a piping tube stand or on a damp cloth to stop the open end drying out.

Happy New Year!

See in Chinese New Year in style and celebrate with a New Year lantern pop at your party. Pipe on personal messages, your guests' names or designs such as hearts.

Valentine Lovehearts

Materials:

Cake pop mixture (see page 48)
Red or pink melting candy
Red and pink modelling paste
Icing sugar
Piping gel
Lollipop sticks

Tools:

Measuring spoons
Polystyrene block
Non-stick board
Non-stick rolling pin, 23cm (9in)
Palette knife
Paintbrush
Heart cutters: 3cm (1⅛in), 2.5cm
   (1in), 2cm (¾in)
Medium heart plunger, 1cm (⅜in)
Greaseproof paper
Baking tray

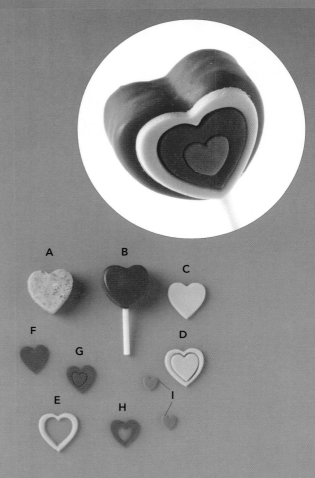

Instructions:

1 Prepare the cake pop (A) following the technique on page 48 for 'Making different shapes' using the 3cm (1⅛) heart cutter.

2 Prepare some red melting candy and secure the lollipop stick to the pop following the technique on page 48. Make sure the lollipop stick is pushed into the point end of the heart shape. Chill flat on greaseproof paper on a baking tray in the fridge.

3 Dip each heart pop into the red melted candy (see page 48) and return to the fridge to set (B).

4 Roll out some pink modelling paste, thinly, on a non-stick board, making sure the paste is free moving on the surface. Stamp out a pink heart (C) using the 2.5cm (1in) cutter.

5 Use the 2cm (¾in) heart cutter, and cut out a shape inside the larger heart (D). Discard the pink heart inside to leave a hollow heart (E).

6 Repeat this technique with red modelling paste and using the 2cm (¾in) cutter (F), then use the 1cm (⅜in) heart plunger to remove the inside of this shape (G). Discard the red heart inside to leave a hollow heart (H).

7 Knead a little pink and red modelling paste together, about half and half, to make a salmon pink colour. Roll out the mixed paste and cut out a heart shape using the heart plunger (I). Any extra shapes can be used for decoration if required.

8 Place all the hearts inside each other, neatly, in order of size. Brush a little piping gel on to the dipped heart pop and use a palette knife to lift and place the concentric hearts into the centre of the pop. Use a palette knife to adjust their position before smoothing with your finger to secure. Leave to dry in a polystyrene block.

Tips!

*Use a little icing sugar to prevent the paste from sticking to your board, but be sparing – too much will dry out the paste.

*Moving the cutter from side to side slightly when cutting out the paste will help give a clean cut edge.

Sweetheart

To make a simpler heart pop, follow instructions 1–4, dipping your heart pop in the melted candy colour of your choice, and stick on a heart-themed sweet with a little piping gel.

Valentine Chocolate Cake

Materials:

Cake pop mixture (see page 48)

Cocoa melting candy

Chocolate (brown) buttercream/frosting

Sugar sprinkles in pink

Rice paper

Pink modelling paste

Piping gel

Edible lustre sprays in gold and pink

Lollipop sticks

Tools:

Polystyrene block

Disposable piping bag

No. 42c piping tube

Non-stick rolling pin, 23cm (9in)

Heart cutter: 3cm (1⅛)

Circle cutter: 5cm (2in)

Blossom plunger 1cm (⅜in)

Non-stick board

Small scissors

Decorative craft scissors (optional)

Scallop tool/spoon

Greaseproof paper

Baking tray

Pencil

Instructions:

1 Prepare the cake pop (A) following the technique on page 48 for 'Making different shapes' using the 3cm (1⅛) heart cutter.

2 Prepare some cocoa melting candy and secure the lollipop stick to the pop following the technique on page 48. Make sure the stick is inserted into the middle of the flat base of the heart shape and be careful not to push it in too far. Chill flat on greaseproof paper on a baking tray in the fridge.

3 Dip each heart pop into the cocoa melting candy (see page 48) and return to the fridge to set (B).

Tip!

Don't use the lustre spray too closely to the rice paper as it will get too wet.

4 Place a 5cm (2in) circle cutter on to a piece of rice paper and use a pencil to draw around it. Use plain or decorative craft scissors to cut out the shape and snip a small 'x' to create a hole in the centre, or use a hole punch. Spray the rice paper with a mixture of pink and gold lustre sprays and leave to dry (C).

5 Thread the coloured rice paper circle on to the prepared cake pop stick, through the 'x' or hole, and secure with a little buttercream (D).

6 Cut off the end of a disposable piping bag and place a no. 42c piping tube inside. Fill with a little buttercream of a medium consistency. Pipe a line (E) along the top and base edges of the cake. Touch the piping tube to the pop, apply pressure to the bag, lift slightly and allow the line of icing to drop on to the pop, whilst turning the stick in the other hand.

7 Paint a little piping gel on to the top of the cake and transfer sugar sprinkles (F) on to the gelled area using a scallop tool or spoon.

8 Roll out some pink modelling paste on a non-stick board and using the 1cm (⅜in) medium blossom plunger, stamp out a number of blossoms (G). Secure these on to the mini cake using a little buttercream. Pipe a buttercream centre (H) in the middle of each one. Leave to dry in a polystyrene block.

Sweet Romance
Get creative and try different piped designs. Add ready-made heart sprinkles for speed and impact.

Mother's Day Flowers

Materials:

Cake pop mixture
(see page 48)

Pink melting candy

Food colouring in
pink and black

Rice paper

Chocolate
buttercream/
frosting

Pink buttercream/
frosting

Edible pearls in blush
pink colour

Edible red dust

Piping gel

Pink modelling paste

Pink ribbon

Cookie sticks

Tools:

Measuring spoon (tbsp)

5 petal flower cutter,
7.5cm (3in)

Blossom plunger, 1cm
(⅜in)

Disposable piping bags

No. 2 piping tube

Tweezers

Paintbrush

Small scissors

Polystyrene block

Kitchen paper

Non-stick rolling pin,
23cm (9in)

Pencil

Instructions:

1 Roll a tablespoon of cake pop mixture
into a ball. Repeat for as many pops as you
require and allow them to set by chilling in
the fridge.

2 Prepare some pink melting candy and
secure the cookie stick to the pop
following the technique on page 48. Place
into a polystyrene block and chill in the fridge.

3 Dip each flowerhead pop into the pink melted
candy (see page 48) and return to the fridge to set (A).

4 Prepare some black and some pink buttercream, following the technique
on page 9, step 6. Cut off the end of a disposable piping bag and place a
no. 2 piping tube inside. Fill the bag with black buttercream and pipe on two
eyes. Prepare another piping bag and fill with the pink buttercream to pipe
on nose and mouth (B).

5 Place the 5 petal flower cutter on to rice paper and draw around it with
a pencil, then cut out the shape (C). Use a little melted candy to secure the
rice paper blossom to the cake pop and leave to dry flat.

6 Roll out pink modelling paste fairly thinly and using the 1cm (⅜in) medium blossom plunger, cut out the blossoms (D). Secure these on to the cake pop in a semi-circle to frame the face, using a little piping gel. Add a dot of buttercream to each blossom centre (E). Use tweezers to place an edible pearl in the centre of each one (F). Leave to dry flat.

7 Dip a paintbrush into some edible red dust, tap off the excess on to a piece of kitchen paper and lightly add blusher to the cheeks of the face in a circular movement (G).

8 Tie a length of ribbon in a bow around the top of the cookie stick to finish.

Pretty Petals

Use modelling paste instead of rice paper to make the petals. Roll them out very thinly and leave to dry in a former or bowl to give them more shape, and add movement by ball tooling the edges. You can change the petal colours and pipe a message on to the flower centre instead of a face.

Easter Bunny

Materials:

Cake pop mixture (see page 48)

Cocoa melting candy

White melting candy

Tiny amounts of pink and chocolate (brown) buttercream/frosting

Food colouring in pink and black

White modelling paste

Pink modelling paste

Ribbon

Lollipop or cookie sticks

Rice paper

Piping gel

Tools:

Measuring spoon (tbsp)

Non-stick rolling pin, 23cm (9in)

Non-stick board

Disposable piping bag

No. 2 piping tube

Dresden tool

Scriber or cocktail stick

Polystyrene block

Gerbera plunger, 8.5 cm (3¼in)

Instructions:

1 Roll a tablespoon measurement of cake pop mixture into a ball between the palms of your hands (A). Shape to a triangle, by pinching between your index finger and thumb (B). Repeat for as many pops as you require and allow them to set by chilling in the fridge.

2 Prepare some white melting candy and secure the lollipop or cookie stick to the pop following the technique on page 48. Place into a polystyrene block and chill in the fridge.

3 Dip each bunny head pop into the white melted candy (see page 48) and return to the fridge to set.

4 Roll out some white modelling paste thinly on the non-stick board, and using the 8.5cm (3¼in) Gerbera plunger, cut out the shape. Move the cutter from side to side whilst pressing down to encourage a clean cut (C). One petal will equal one ear, so divide the petals by cutting with a scriber (D).

5 To make the centre of the bunny's ears, roll a very small amount of pink modelling paste into a ball and then roll into a thin sausage shape (E). To attach it to the centre of the ear, put it into position on one of the gerbera petals using the flat end of the Dresden tool (F). Flatten and smooth it by pressing it gently using your index finger in the palm of your hand from the tip and down the centre (G). Repeat this process for the other ear and secure them to the head with a little melted candy or piping gel.

6 To make the bunny's cheeks, roll a dragee-sized ball of modelling paste (H) between your finger and thumb to create a teardrop shape (I). Flatten it slightly and add texture using the Dresden tool by lightly dragging it through the paste to create whiskers (J). Add a number of whisker holes using the scriber or cocktail stick. Repeat for the other cheek.

7 Cut out two tiny rectangles of rice paper for the teeth and attach where the two cheeks meet with a little piping gel (K).

8 Roll a half dragee-sized amount of white modelling paste into a ball to make an eyeball.

9 Prepare a tiny amount of pink and black buttercream, following the technique on page 9, step 6. Cut off the end of a disposable piping bag and place a no. 2 piping tube inside. Fill the bag with black buttercream and pipe on the pupil for each eyeball. Prepare another piping bag and half fill with the pink buttercream to pipe on the nose.

10 Tie a length of ribbon in a bow around the top of the cookie stick to finish and leave to dry in the polystyrene block.

Rabbits in the Headlights!
Make the bunnies look shocked by using ready-made candy eyeballs. Change their colour and ear position for a different look.

Easter Chick

Materials:

Cake pop mixture (see page 48)

Yellow melting candy

Orange modelling paste

Edible red dust

Piping gel

Chocolate (brown) buttercream/frosting

Black food colouring

Cookie sticks

Tools:

Measuring spoon (tbsp)

Non-stick rolling pin, 23cm (9in)

Non-stick board

Disposable piping bags

Small scissors

Dresden tool or cocktail stick

Paintbrush

Heart cutter: 2cm (¾in)

Kitchen paper

Polystyrene block

Instructions:

1 Roll a tablespoon and a half measurement of cake pop mixture into a ball between the palms of your hands (A). Make a second, smaller cake pop ball from one tablespoon of cake pop mixture (B).

2 Prepare some yellow melting candy and secure the larger pop (the chick's body) to the cookie stick following the technique on page 48. Leave enough of the stick exposed to attach the smaller cake pop ball – the chick's head. Place into a polystyrene block and chill in the fridge.

3 When chilled, secure the smaller head pop as described above and following the technique on page 48 (C). This is a bi-pop. Repeat for as many pops as you require and allow them to set by chilling in the fridge.

4 Dip the whole bi-pop in yellow melting candy (see page 48) and return to the fridge to set.

5 Roll out some orange modelling paste, quite thinly, on a non-stick board and cut out two feet using the 2cm (¾in) heart cutter (D). Using a Dresden tool or cocktail stick, mark five lines on the paste to add detail to the feet (E). Repeat for the other foot and secure them either side of the stick, on to the chick's lower body, using a little piping gel.

6 To make the beak, roll a dragee-sized piece of orange modelling paste into a ball (F). Roll into a sausage shape with tapered ends by rolling between your finger and thumb first at one end, then the other (G).

7 Brush a little piping gel on to the chick's head ready to attach the beak. Place the Dresden tool or cocktail stick horizontally across the middle of the beak, and press it on to the chick's head (H).

8 Melt some yellow candy, place it into a disposable piping bag and snip the end off. Pipe wings and tail feathers on to the chick by using semi-circular motions to create a fluted pattern. Pipe a dot on to the top of the head and pull upwards, easing the pressure off as you lift away, to form head feathers.

9 Dip a paintbrush into the edible red dust, tap off the excess into a sheet of kitchen paper and dust lightly across the chick's cheeks.

10 Prepare some black buttercream following the method on page 9, step 6. Using a disposable piping bag and a no. 2 piping tube, pipe on two dots for the eyes. Leave to dry in a polystyrene block.

Chick Chums

These cute chicks work well in a variety of colours. The chick at the front was dipped in pink melting candy, and his beak is a ready-made triangle-shaped sugar sprinkle, which could also be used for feet. Faster and still just as fun!

Tip!
Don't be tempted to use lollipop sticks or plastic straws for bi-pops! Cookie sticks are much thicker and stronger and can hold the extra weight and size.

Father's Day Cars

Materials:

Cake pop mixture
(see page 48)

Red melting candy

Black modelling
paste

Dragees in red

Piping gel

Chocolate (brown)
buttercream/
frosting

Black food colouring

Chocolate sprinkles

Lollipop sticks

Tools:

Measuring spoon (tbsp)

Non-stick board

Non-stick rolling pin,
23cm (9in)

No. 17 piping tube (used
as a circle cutter)

Square cutter: 1.5 cm
(½in)

Palette knife

Ball tool

Paintbrush

No. 2 piping tube

Disposable piping bag

Scriber or cocktail stick

Polystyrene block

Tweezers

Small scissors

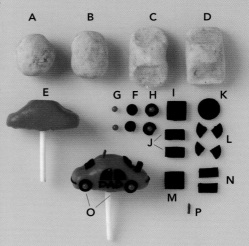

Instructions:

1 Roll a tablespoon of cake pop mixture into
a ball (A). Shape to an oval, using your finger
and thumb (B). Place on the non-stick board
and using your a finger at each end of the oval,
press down and indent the oval cake pop to
create a bonnet and boot of the car (C). Flatten
the sides, by pressing a palette knife each
side (D).

2 Prepare some red melting candy and secure
the lollipop stick to the car pop following the
technique on page 48. Place into a polystyrene
block and chill in the fridge.

3 Dip each car pop into the red melted candy
(see page 48) and return to the fridge to set (E).

4 Roll out some black modelling paste, but
not too thinly. Using a no. 17 piping tube as a
circle cutter, stamp out four wheels (F). Put the
paste in a bag to prevent it drying out. Indent
the centres of each wheel with the small end of
a ball tool. Use tweezers to drop a red dragee
(G) into the wheel centres, securing in place
with piping gel (H). Use piping gel to attach the
wheels to the car pop.

> **Tip!**
> Spray edible pearl
> lustre into the can lid
> and use as a paint to
> add highlights to the
> windscreen.

5 Take the paste out of the bag, cut out a square with the 1.5 cm (½in) cutter (I), and cut in half (J) to make two spoilers. Secure one to the rear of the car and use the other for another car.

6 Still using the rolled-out black paste, cut out a circle with the large end of the piping tube (K) and divide it into four equal parts (L). Cut out another square with the 1.5cm (½in) cutter (M), cut in half, and use for the front and rear windows (N). Secure in place with a small amount of piping gel.

7 Add 2 tablespoons of black food colouring to the chocolate buttercream to make it black. Cut off the end of a disposable piping bag and place a no. 2 piping tube inside. Part fill the bag with the prepared buttercream. Pipe a smile on to the front of the car and any lettering (O).

8 Use a scriber or cocktail stick to make a tiny hole on top of the car roof to hold the aerial. Using tweezers, dip a chocolate sprinkle in a little piping gel before pushing carefully into the hole (P).

Top Gear

Change the car colour to make your dad's dream car and make his wish come true. Simplify by omitting the wording and the aerial.

Halloween Witch

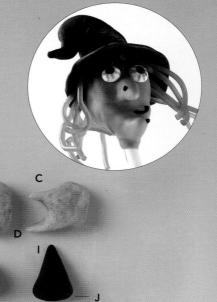

Materials:

Cake pop mixture (see page 48)

Green melting candy

Black modelling paste

Chocolate (brown) buttercream/ frosting

Blue and yellow moon and stars sprinkles

Red strawberry lace sweets

Piping gel

Candy eyeballs

Edible ink pen in red/ red food colour

Cookie sticks

Tools:

Measuring spoon (tbsp)

Disposable piping bag

Tweezers

Polystyrene block

Small scissors

Instructions:

1 Roll a tablespoon of cake pop mixture into a ball (A), then carefully shape to an oval, between your finger and thumb (B). With your fingers, pinch out a nose to a sharp point in the centre of the oval (C). Form the chin, by easing the other end of the oval to a point in the same way as the nose (D).

2 Prepare some green melting candy. Secure the cookie stick to the witch's head, by inserting it into the centre base of the pop just behind the chin, following the technique on page 48 (E). Place into a polystyrene block and chill in the fridge.

3 Dip each witch's head pop into the green melted candy (see page 48) and return to the fridge to set (F).

4 For the hair, secure strips of strawberry lace sweets in place with buttercream or melting candy and leave to set upright in a polystyrene block (G).

5 To make the hat, roll a grape-sized amount of modelling paste into a ball (H). Model it into a cone shape by rolling in the palms of your hands at one end (I). Flatten the base of the wide end of the cone (J).

6 Make a brim by pushing your thumb up into the base of the hat. Use your finger to ease and smooth the paste over the thumb to form a brim (K). Roll the tip of the hat between your finger and thumb to a point and bend to one side for movement (L). Add a ready-made star from the sprinkles for decoration and glue it in place with piping gel. Secure the hat in place with buttercream.

7 Draw lines on to the candy eyeballs with an edible ink pen and secure in place with a little gel, using the tweezers to position them (M). Pipe on a mouth, and a brown wart on the chin and nose, using brown buttercream in a disposable piping bag with the end snipped off.

Magical Wizard

Make a wizard in the same way without pointing the nose downwards. His hair, beard and moustache are piped with a no. 42c piping tube. His hat is a simple blue cone and has both moon and star sprinkles.

Halloween Pumpkin

Materials:

Cake pop mixture (see page 48)

Orange melting candy

Green modelling paste

Very small amount of yellow modelling paste

Edible red dust

Piping gel

Brown buttercream/frosting

Black food colouring

Lollipop sticks

Tools:

Measuring spoon (tbsp)

Paintbrush

Disposable piping bag

No. 2 piping tube

Cutting wheel tool

Polystyrene block

Instructions:

1 Roll a tablespoon of cake pop mixture into a ball between the palms of your hands (A). Flatten slightly to form an oval, between your finger and thumb (B). Mark lines on the top of the pop by rolling the small end of a cutting wheel tool from the centre outwards; these will show through after dipping. Repeat for as many pops as you require and allow them to set by chilling in the fridge.

2 Prepare some orange melting candy and secure the lollipop stick to the pop following the technique on page 48. Place into a polystyrene block and chill in the fridge.

3 Dip each pumpkin pop into the orange melted candy (see page 48) and return to the fridge to set (C).

4 Roll a pea-sized ball of green paste (D) into a cylindrical shape (E) using your finger and thumb. Secure to the centre of the pumpkin with piping gel. Take two more pea-sized amounts of green paste and roll them into thin sausage shapes for the tendrils (F). Twist and attach these with piping gel.

5 Roll a very tiny dragee-sized ball (G) of yellow paste into a teardrop shape (H) and secure to the top of the stalk to look like a candle flame.

6 Use black coloured buttercream (see page 9, step 6) and a no. 2 piping tube in a piping bag to pipe on spooky eyes, nose and a crooked, zigzag smile.

7 When the piping is dry, dust a little edible red dust using a paintbrush across the yellow paste flame. Leave to dry fully in the polystyrene block.

Big Fright!

Make a bigger pumpkin by adding an extra tablespoon of the mixture. Make them just as spooky, but quicker to make by omitting the paste flame and the tendrils.

Tip!
Thicken melting candy by adding very small amounts of water.

Christmas Snowman

Materials:

Cake pop mix (see page 48)

White melting candy

Pale blue modelling paste

Orange modelling paste

Piping gel

Edible red dust

Black-coloured buttercream/
frosting

Edible lustre spray in pearl

Tools:

Measuring spoon (tbsp)

Non-stick board

Non-stick rolling pin 23cm
(9in)

Disposable piping bag

Cookie sticks

Cocktail stick

Circle cutter: 3.5cm (1¼in)

Square cutter: 5cm (2in)

Sharp knife

Kitchen paper

No. 2 piping tube

Soft dusting brush

Polystyrene block

Food bag

Ball tool

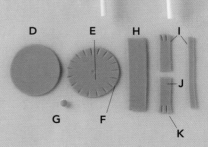

Instructions:

1 Roll a tablespoon and a half measurement of cake pop mixture into a ball between the palms of your hands. Make a second, smaller cake pop ball from one tablespoon of cake pop mixture.

2 Prepare some white melting candy and secure the larger pop (the snowman's body) to the cookie stick following the technique on page 48 (A). Leave enough of the stick exposed to attach the smaller cake pop ball – the snowman's head. Place into a polystyrene block and chill in the fridge.

3 When chilled, secure the smaller head pop as described above and following the technique on page 48 (B). This is a bi-pop. Repeat for as many pops as you require and allow them to set by chilling in the fridge.

4 Dip the whole bi-pop in white melting candy (see page 48) and return to the fridge to set (C).

5 Roll out some blue modelling paste on the non-stick board, and cut out a circle using the 3.5cm (1¼in) circle cutter (D). Place the remaining rolled-out paste in a food bag until later. Indent the centre with the small end of a ball tool (E). Mark the outside edge of the circle with short lines using a cocktail stick (F).

6 Make a dragee-sized ball out of blue paste for the hat bobble and secure with piping gel into the centre indentation of the blue circle (G).

7 Take the paste out of the bag and cut out a rectangle, by using the square cutter to cut the basic shape (H) and then dividing this in half (I). Use one half as the scarf wrapped around the snowman's neck and trim to fit. Cut the second half in half again for the two ends of the scarf (J). Use a knife to cut vertical lines at the end of the two strips for the tassels (K), and secure the two ends of the scarf first, then wrap around the neck.

8 Roll a dragee-sized ball of orange paste into a cone shape by rolling between your finger and thumb at one end. Secure to the snowman's face with a little piping gel.

9 Place a little edible dust on to a piece of kitchen paper, load a brush with the dust, tap off the excess and apply to the snowman's cheeks in a circular motion.

10 Prepare a disposable piping bag with a no. 2 piping tube and fill with black buttercream. Pipe on two eyes, a mouth and three buttons. When fully dry, add a little edible lustre spray in pearl to make him shimmer.

Speedy Snowman

To make a slightly different snowman, omit the scarf. Pipe twig arms and maybe use a red dragee instead of a carrot nose; this will be a little quicker but just as cute!

Christmas Pudding

Materials:

Cake pop mixture (see page 48)

Dark cocoa melting candy

White modelling paste

Edible lustre spray in pearl

Piping gel

Ready-made holly leaf and berry sprinkles

Lollipop or cookie sticks

Tools:

Measuring spoon (tbsp)

Fluted circle cutter, 2.5cm (1in)

Soft dusting brush

Paintbrush

Tweezers

Kitchen paper

Polystyrene block

Non-stick board

Non-stick rolling pin 23cm (9in)

Instructions:

1 Roll a tablespoon of cake pop mixture into a ball between the palms of your hands. Repeat for as many pops as you require and allow them to set by chilling in the fridge.

2 Prepare some dark cocoa melting candy and secure the lollipop stick to the pop following the technique on page 48. Place into a polystyrene block and chill in the fridge.

3 Dip each pudding pop into the dark cocoa melted candy (see page 48) and return to the fridge to set (A).

4 Make the white sauce effect by rolling out white modelling paste fairly thinly on a non-stick board. Cut out a wavy-edged circle using the 2.5cm (1in) fluted circle cutter (B).

5 Place on to kitchen paper and dust with dry edible lustre spray dust in pearl, using a soft dusting brush (C). Paint piping gel on to the reverse of the dusted wavy-edged circle and secure to the pudding (D).

6 Use tweezers to dip three holly leaf and three berry sprinkles into piping gel and then arrange them in the centre of the pudding (E). Leave to dry in the polystyrene block.

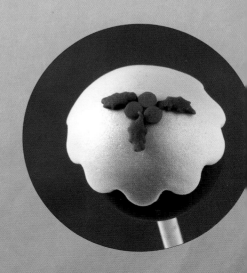

Festive Treats

Try making these puds bigger or omit the sauce and pipe on a flame instead. Pour melted candy into a disposable bag, snip of the end and pipe a large dot on to greaseproof paper. Pull a paintbrush from the centre of the candy outwards and leave to set in the fridge. Secure with buttercream at the back to support.

Tip:

Spray edible pearl lustre into the can lid or on to some kitchen paper, leave to dry and use as a dust.

Fat Christmas Robin

Materials:

Cake pop mixture (see page 48)
Cocoa melting candy
Red modelling paste
Piping gel
Yellow modelling paste
Chocolate sprinkles
Brown buttercream/frosting
Black food colouring
Cookie sticks

Tools:

Measuring spoon (tbsp)
Small scissors
Scriber or cocktail stick
Tweezers
Disposable piping bag
No. 2 piping tube
Circle cutter: 3.2cm (1¼in)
Polystyrene block
Non-stick board
Non-stick rolling pin 23cm (9in)

A   B   C

D   E   F

Instructions:

1 Roll two tablespoons of cake pop mixture into a ball between the palms of your hands. Repeat for as many pops as you require and allow them to set by chilling in the fridge.

2 Prepare some cocoa melting candy and secure the lollipop stick to the pop following the technique on page 48 (A). Place into a polystyrene block and chill in the fridge.

3 Use a small pair of narrow-ended scissors and carefully snip two wings and a tail into the set cake pop. Be sure not to cut too deeply or they will break off when dipping (B).

4 Dip each robin pop into the cocoa melted candy (see page 48) and return to the fridge to set (C).

5 Roll out some red modelling paste fairly thinly on to a non-stick board. Using the 3.5cm (1¼in) circle cutter, cut out a circle, to make the red breast (D). Position this to the front of the pop and secure with piping gel, leaving enough room for the beak.

6 For the beak, take a pea-sized ball of yellow modelling paste and roll it to a cone shape between your finger and thumb (E). Slightly flatten it at the same time, then secure it above the breast with piping gel.

7 Make leg holes, one on each side of the pop, by carefully inserting a scriber or cocktail stick just a little way into the pop. Use tweezers to pick up each sprinkle, dip it in the gel and push it gently into the hole. Repeat for each leg (F).

8 Pipe on two dots for the eyes using black buttercream made by adding black food colouring to brown buttercream/frosting and a no. 2 piping tube in a piping bag. Leave to dry in a polystyrene block.

Cocoa Cutie
Make a different-sized robin by changing the measurement of cake pop mixture. Leave out the wings and legs for a simpler but still cute and cuddly bird.

Tip!
To make the robin's beak look open, use a pair of scissors to cut a line and ease open gently to make a squawking bird.

Engagement Rings

Materials:

Cake pop mixture (see page 48)

Red melting candy

Piping gel

White and pink modelling paste

Edible pearls

Edible lustre spray in gold

Lollipop sticks

Tools:

Measuring spoon (tbsp)

Tweezers

Blossom plunger, 1cm (⅜in)

Non-stick rolling pin, 23cm (9in)

Non-stick board

Smoother

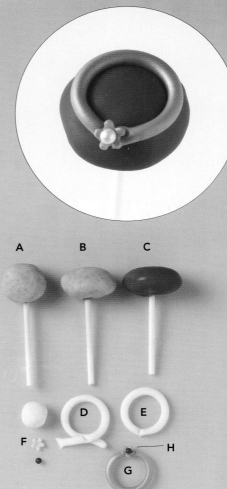

Instructions:

1 Roll a tablespoon of cake pop mixture into a ball between the palms of your hands (A). Flatten slightly to form an oval by lightly pinching all around the edge, between your finger and thumb. Repeat for as many pops as you require and allow them to set by chilling in the fridge.

2 Prepare some red melting candy and secure the lollipop stick to the pop following the technique on page 48 (B). Place into a polystyrene block and chill in the fridge.

3 Dip each engagement pop into the red melted candy (see page 48) and return to the fridge to set (C).

4 Roll a large pea-sized ball of white modelling paste into a sausage shape by rolling it on to the board using your fingers at first, and then a smoother to neaten out the bumps. Be sure not to push too hard, or the sausage shape will become too flat. Roll to and fro gently along the length of the paste sausage.

5 Wrap the paste sausage into a circular shape (you can use a circle cutter as a guide if it helps). Overlap the ends and cut through both of them (D).

6 Remove the surplus paste and join the ends together (E).

7 Roll out some pink modelling paste and using the 1cm (⅜in) blossom plunger, cut out a blossom (F).

8 Secure the blossom with piping gel on to the ring of paste, covering the join and spray with edible gold lustre (G). Allow to dry.

9 Attach the paste ring to the red pop cushion and use tweezers to drop an edible pearl into the centre of the blossom, securing with piping gel (H). Leave to dry in the polystyrene block.

Candy Gems

Try a different look by using colourful jelly beans to look like precious stones. Change the colour of the edible spray and add sprinkles to edge the pop for extra sparkle and bling!

Tip!

Any melted candy drips that are left on the sticks can be wiped away easily with a damp cloth without leaving any marks. A thin ribbon tied on at the base of the pop will also neaten any unevenness.

Bride & Groom

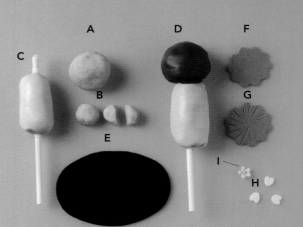

Materials:

Cake pop mixture (see page 48)

White and pink or brown melting candy

Black, brown and pink modelling pastes

Brown buttercream/frosting

Black food colouring

Piping gel

Edible pearl

Cookie sticks

Tools:

Measuring spoon (tbsp)

Oval cutter: 7cm (2¾in)

Knife

Bulbous cone tool/cocktail stick

Fluted circle cutter, 2.5cm (1in)

Cutting wheel

Heart plunger, 6mm (¼in)

Blossom plunger, 1cm (⅜in)

Disposable piping bags

No. 2 piping tube

Non-stick board

Non-stick rolling pin, 23cm (9in)

Polystyrene block

Instructions:

1 To make the groom: roll a tablespoon of cake pop mixture into a long oval shape by rolling in the middle of the palm of your hand. Make a second, smaller cake pop ball for the head (A). Prepare some white melting candy and secure the lollipop stick to the pop following the technique on page 48, leaving enough of the stick exposed to attach the head. The bride at this stage would require a small ball of cake mixture to be cut in half and attached with a little melted candy before dipping, for the bust (B). Place into a polystyrene block and chill in the fridge.

2 Dip each body pop into the white melted candy (see page 48) and return to the fridge to set (C). Attach the head, dip in pink or brown melted candy and return to the fridge to set (D).

3 On a non-stick board, roll out some black modelling paste fairly thinly and using the 7cm (2¾in) oval cutter, cut out the shape for the groom's coat (E). Make a small incision on the middle of one edge to create tails. Paint piping gel on to the underside of the shape and attach it to the body, high enough to be able to curl the paste over at the neck to make a collar.

4 Add two buttonholes to the groom's coat with a bulbous cone tool or by pushing a cocktail stick into the paste.

5 Roll out some brown modelling paste and make the hair by cutting a shape with the 2.5cm (1in) fluted circle cutter (F). Add texture to the hair with a cutting wheel by rolling the wheel from the centre to the outside of the shape (G). Secure to the head with melted candy.

6 Roll out some pink modelling paste and cut out three heart shapes using the 6mm (¼in) plunger, and a blossom shape with the 1cm (⅜in) blossom plunger (H). Mark the hearts with a cocktail stick to make fold lines on the bow tie. Attach two of the hearts, on their sides with their points touching, under the groom's chin for the bow tie. Roll the third heart into an oval shape and place between the hearts for the knot. Secure them all with piping gel. Attach the blossom to the lapel of the groom's jacket and place an edible pearl in the centre using buttercream or piping gel as glue (I).

7 Using brown buttercream coloured with black food colouring, pipe on two dots for the eyes and a 'U' shape for the mouth, using a no. 2 piping tube in a piping bag. Pipe on the ears and nose in the same way using brown melting candy. Leave to dry in the polystyrene block.

Wedded Bliss

The bride is made in the same way as the groom; her dress is made using the same sized oval cutter, but using the fluted side to cut it out. A textured rolling pin creates a pretty design on the dress: roll it across the modelling paste to emboss, keeping an even pressure. Pipe on her hair using a piping bag with a very small hole in the end cut off, filled with melted candy. Use a small oval cutter to make the veil, add the flower to her hair and finish with edible lustre spray for a romantic shimmer. The groom here also has piped hair, and the flower on his lapel matches his bride's.

Wedding Cake

Materials:

Cake pop mixture (see page 48)

White melting candy

Pink modelling paste

Piping gel

Cookie sticks

Tools:

Greaseproof paper

Non-stick rolling pin, 23cm (9in)

Deep circle cutters: 5cm (2in), 4cm (1½in), 2.5cm (1in)

Paintbrush

Smoother

Non-stick board

Heart plunger, 6mm (¼in)

Tweezers

Polystyrene block

Knife

Elastic band

Pop wrap

Baking tray

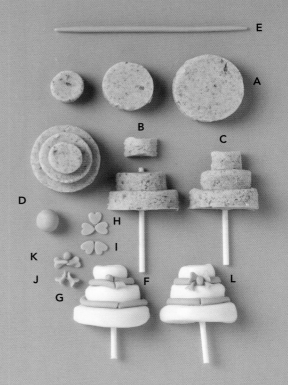

Instructions:

1 Roll out some cake pop mixture following the 'Making different shapes' technique on page 48.

2 Use the three different sizes of deep circle cutter to cut out three shapes.

3 With a little melted candy, glue together the two larger cake circles and before they dry fully, push the dipped cookie stick through the centre, making sure the tip is just protruding (B), enough to attach the smallest cake circle on to the top. Use a little melted candy to help glue the circles together. The cake circles need to be placed centrally one on top of the other (C). Leave to set and chill upside down on greaseproof paper on a baking tray, with the stick uppermost, for at least two hours. Dip it in white melting candy and chill for six hours following the basic technique on page 48.

4 When set, attach a pop wrap underneath, securing it in place with an elastic band to prevent slipping and help to support the tri-pop.

5 Roll a pea-sized ball, of pink modelling paste (D) into a sausage shape(E), on a non-stick board. Use your fingers to start with, then neaten it when the correct length is reached using the smoother. Take care not to flatten it. This will be a sugar ribbon.

6 Place the ribbon of paste around the top tier (F), overlap the ends, and cut through both pieces. Remove the excess paste to allow the ends to join together neatly. Now the ends can be secured together with piping gel. You may find it easier to pick the pop up to work on instead of leaving it in the polystyrene block. Repeat for the next tier.

7 Roll out pink modelling paste and cut out five small hearts (H), using the plunger cutter.

8 The two lower hearts (I), will make the tails. Pinch the point of each heart between finger and thumb (J). Press the two heart points together. Tweezers may help with this.

9 Pinch the points of the next two heart shapes to make left and right bows (K). Make a ball of pink modelling paste for the centre of the bow. Secure the tails, bow and centre to the ribbon join with piping gel (L). Make two more bows and secure one to the other ribbon and one on top of the cake.

Piece of Cake!

The other beautiful cake has been made using lilac-coloured modelling paste instead. You can change the colour to suit the theme of the wedding you are celebrating.

Fairy

Tools:

Measuring spoon (tbsp)

Palette knife

Disposable piping bags

Star plunger, 1cm (⅜ in)

Ruffle pop wrap

Elastic band

Non-stick rolling pin, 23cm (9in)

Paintbrush

Heart cutter: 2.5cm (1in)

No. 2 piping tube

Polystyrene block

Small scissors

Blossom plungers, 1cm (⅜in), 1.3cm (½in)

Materials:

Cake pop mixture (see page 48)

Pink and yellow melting candy

Pink, white and yellow modelling paste

Cookie sticks

Edible lustre spray in blue

Brown and pink buttercream/frosting

Black food colouring

Edible pearls

Piping gel

Instructions:

1 Roll a tablespoon of cake pop mixture into a ball (A), then model into an oval by lightly shaping between finger and thumb.

2 Place on to the work surface and press lightly with a palette knife to flatten the base (B).

3 Dip the stick as shown on page 48. Ease the pop on to the stick, smoothing it into a triangle. Leave the top of the stick a little exposed. Dip in yellow melting candy (C). Leave to chill in a polystyrene block.

4 Measure half a tablespoon of cake pop mixture and roll into a ball (D). Dip the protruding stick, attach the pop and chill, then cover in pink melting candy (see page 48). This is a bi-pop.

5 Pour melted yellow candy into a disposable piping bag and snip the end off. Touch the pop head with the end of the bag, apply light pressure and use an up and down motion to pipe the hair (E). At the same time pipe a wand, in the centre of the body (F).

6 Use the same procedure to pipe a dot for the nose (G), and two lines for the arms, either side of the wand in pink melted candy.

7 Cut two shapes, using the heart cutter from rolled-out white modelling paste and leave to dry. When fully dry, spray with edible blue lustre (H).

8 Roll out pink modelling paste quite thinly and cut out a large blossom (I) and a small blossom. Add an edible pearl to the centre of the smallest blossom and use a paintbrush to secure it with piping gel (J). Secure this to the larger blossom (K), and attach it to the fairy's head.

9 Roll out yellow modelling paste and use the star plunger to stamp out a star (L). Attach it to the end of the wand. Pipe two dots for the eyes with brown buttercream coloured with black food colouring, using the no. 2 piping tube, and a 'u' shape for a mouth with pink buttercream. Leave to dry.

10 Attach a pop wrap (M), when dry. Secure it with an elastic band pushed up underneath to prevent slipping. Lastly, secure the two blue hearts in place as wings, using leftover melting candy.

Flower Power
Make a slightly different fairy by dipping the body and head in different colours. Make the blossoms in a variety of colours and add fairy dust made from lustre spray or glitter flakes. Magical!

Robot

Materials:

Cake pop mixture (see page 48)

Cocoa melting candy

Jelly beans

Edible lustre spray in silver

Red modelling paste

Dragees in red

Brown buttercream/ frosting

Black food colouring

Piping gel

Lollipop sticks

Cornflour

Tools:

Deep square cutter, 4cm (1½in)

No. 18 piping tube (used as a circle cutter)

Palette knife

Ball tool

No. 2 piping tube

Disposable piping bag

Non-stick board

Non-stick rolling pin, 23cm (9in)

Polystyrene block

Sharp knife

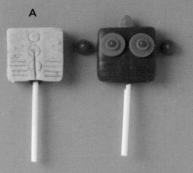

A

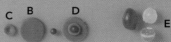

C   B   D

E

Instructions:

1 Roll out the cake pop mixture using the 'Making different shapes' technique on page 48. Use the deep square cutter. Attach the lollipop stick as described on page 48, pushing the stick into the side of the shape. Indent circles with the no. 18 piping tube and lines with a palette knife (A).

2 Dip in cocoa melting candy and chill: see the technique on page 48.

3 Make the robot's eyes by rolling out red modelling paste quite thinly on a non-stick board. Use both the top and base of the no. 18 piping tube to cut out a large circle (B), and a small circle (C). Use a little cornflour to prevent the paste sticking inside the piping tube.

4 Indent the centre of the small circle with the small end of a ball tool. Secure a red dragee (D), on the small circle and then secure this on the large circle using piping gel. Repeat with the second eye.

5 Cut a jelly bean in half (E), to make the ears. Cut a second jelly bean in half to make an antenna. Secure them in position with a little melted candy. Leave to dry in a polystyrene block.

6 Spray in silver edible lustre spray, including the stick if desired, and allow to dry.

7 Colour chocolate buttercream with black food colouring and use the no. 2 piping tube and a piping bag to pipe three straight lines in a 'u' shape for the mouth. Leave to dry in polystyrene.

The Future is Pop-Shaped

The ladybot is created by making a round pop, using a single circle of paste for the eyes and modelling a teardrop shape for her antenna. Spray her in red lustre. Adding a mouth is optional.

Blue Teddy

Materials:

Cake pop mixture (see page 48)

Blue melting candy

Brown buttercream/frosting

Black food colouring

Blue modelling paste

Lollipop sticks

Piping gel

Tools:

Measuring spoon (tbsp)

Heart plunger, 6mm (¼in)

Disposable piping bag

No. 2 piping tube

Dresden tool or cocktail stick

Polystyrene block

Sharp knife

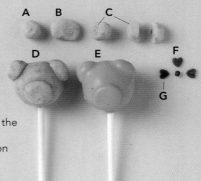

Instructions:

1 Roll a tablespoon of cake pop mixture into a ball between the palms of your hands. Prepare some blue melting candy and secure the lollipop stick to the pop following the technique on page 48, but don't chill yet.

2 Roll a pea-sized amount of mixture into a ball (A), flatten it slightly with your finger to make a muzzle (B), and secure with melted candy to the round teddy head pop.

3 For the ears, roll another pea-sized amount of mixture into a ball and cut in half (C). Secure the flat side to each side of the pop with melted candy (D).

4 Chill to set, and then dip each pop in blue melting candy and return to the fridge to chill, following the basic technique on page 48 (E).

5 Using the 6mm (¼in) heart plunger, stamp out three heart shapes from rolled-out blue modelling paste (F). Attach two of the hearts, on their sides with their points touching, just in front of the bear's ear. Use gel to secure them and position firmly by pushing in place with a cocktail stick or Dresden tool.

6 Roll the third heart shape into a ball and place in between the other two shapes to create the centre knot of the bow (G). Secure with piping gel.

7 Use brown buttercream coloured with black food colouring and a no. 2 piping tube and piping bag to pipe on two eyes, a dot for the nose, and a shape for the mouth as shown. Leave to dry in the polystyrene block.

Blue for a Boy and Pink for a Girl!

This cute pink teddy is perfect for the birthday girl. Substitute the blue bow for a pink flower by using the blossom plunger and adding a pink edible pearl to the centre.

Dove Pop

Materials:

Cake pop mixture (see page 48)
Edible lustre spray in pearl
White melting candy
White modelling paste
Ready-made candy eyeballs
Piping gel
Lollipop or cookie stick

Tools:

Measuring spoon (tbsp)
Heart cutter, 2.5cm (1in)
Dresden tool
Polystyrene block
Non-stick rolling pin 23cm (9in)
Non-stick board
Paintbrush

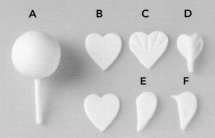

Instructions:

1 Roll a tablespoon of cake pop mixture into a ball between the palms of your hands. Prepare some white melting candy and secure the lollipop stick to the pop following the technique on page 48.

2 Dip each pop in white melting candy and return to the fridge to chill, following the basic technique on page 48 (A).

3 Roll out some white modelling paste on a non-stick board and cut out four heart shapes using the 2.5cm (1in) heart cutter (B).

4 Emboss five lines along the two round heart edges using the sharp end of the Dresden tool (C). Pinch the point of the heart, keeping the lines uppermost. One will make the tail and two more the wings; using a paintbrush secure them all on to the dove's body with a little piping gel (D).

5 Take the fourth heart and fold it centrally in half, squeezing to secure together (E). Pinch the wide end between your finger and thumb to form a beak (F). Secure the beak with piping gel to the front of the pop, flatten it at the base and smooth it to shape the neck.

6 Attach ready-made candy eyeballs either side, using piping gel. Spray with edible lustre spray and leave to dry in the polystyrene block.

Pop of Peace

Coat a round pop in blue spray to make a world and simply add ready-made candy doves with buttercream all around it. World peace in a cake pop!

Champagne Bottle

Materials:

Cake pop mixture (see page 48)

Green melting candy

White modelling paste

Pearl dragee

Edible lustre spray in gold

Piping gel

Edible ink pen in black

Lollipop sticks

Tools:

Measuring spoon (tbsp)

Soft dusting brush

No. 5 piping tube

Paintbrush

Square cutter, 4cm (1½in)

Non-stick rolling pin 23cm (9in)

Non-stick board

Knife

Kitchen paper

Polystyrene block

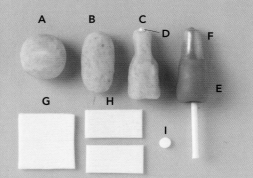

Instructions:

1 Roll a tablespoon of cake pop mixture into a ball between the palms of your hands (A). Shape to an oval, using your finger and thumb (B).

2 Flatten the base by lightly pushing the pop down on to the work surface. Pinch at one end to form a bottle neck and shape the rest of the pop into a bottle shape with your fingers (C). Push a dragee into the top for a cork (D). Repeat for as many pops as you require and allow them to set by chilling in the fridge.

3 Prepare some green melting candy and secure the lollipop stick to the pop following the technique on page 48. Place into a polystyrene block and chill in the fridge.

4 Dip each bottle pop into the green melted candy (see page 48) and return to the fridge to set (E).

5 When chilled, use a soft brush to dust dried edible gold spray on to kitchen paper, then brush it around the neck of the bottle (F).

Tip!
Make sure the modelling paste has dried fully before writing on it with the edible ink pen. You could also change the edible dust colour for a different look.

6 Roll out some white modelling paste fairly thinly, cut out a square using 4cm (1½in) square cutter (G). Divide in half with a knife – this will make two bottle lables (H). Cut out a small circle (I) from another piece of rolled out paste, using the piping end of a no. 5 piping tube.

7 Secure the rectangle and square paste bottle labels to the pop using piping gel and a paintbrush and leave to dry in the polystyrene block.

Party Time!
Write the occasion you are celebrating on to the bottle label with an edible ink pen. Leave the dragee off and pipe a trail of piping gel down the side of the bottle to make it look as though the cork has been popped!

Cake pop re

1 Crumble the sponge either by hand into a bowl or using an electric mixer (preferably with a K beater attachment) until it resembles breadcrumbs.

2 Measure out 1 level cup of buttercream.

3 Combine 6 level cups of cake crumb to the 1 level cup of buttercream (you can add citrus fruit or zest, popping candy or sherbets if desired at this stage) and combine thoroughly. Test that the mixture glues together well. If it is a little dry, add more buttercream.

4 Fill a measuring spoon with the mixture and level out using a palette knife; this will give accurate amounts each time. Different spoon measurements will give different sizes of cake pop.

5 Roll the measured mixture between the palms of your hands to form a round ball. The ball can now be chilled in the fridge to set it. Placing your cake pop balls in the egg holder of your fridge is ideal for this.

Securing the cake pop to a stick

6 Melt the melting candy in the microwave, using bursts of 30 seconds on high to avoid it burning. You can also use a melting pot, or melt it in a bowl over a pan of boiled water.

7 Dip the end of the lollipop stick into the melted candy and push vertically into the cake pop. Place into a polystyrene block and chill in the fridge for about 10 minutes or until the candy has set.

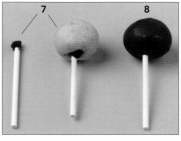

8 Lower the chilled cake pop into the melted candy and twist the stick until the cake pop ball is fully covered; a spoon may help to thoroughly coat it. Lift the cake pop and allow the excess to drip away, tap it lightly on the side of the bowl and roll the stick to remove any drip marks. Push it into polystyrene and chill it in the fridge until set for approximately 10 – 20 minutes.

Making different shapes: Roll out the prepared pop mixture on to greaseproof paper and place between marzipan spacers (deepest side), or deep dowelling. Push a deep-sided cutter into the mixture and cut out your shape. Follow the instructions on this page from stage 6 onwards; the instructions in each project will guide you as to whether to insert the lollipop stick into the side or the top of your shape.